EX LIBRIS

UNIVERSITATIS SANCTI JOANNIS

TWO CHINESE FAMILIES

兩家中国人

Two Chinese Families

by Catherine Edwards Sadler

photographs by Alan Sadler

ATHENEUM   NEW YORK 1981

LIBRARY OF CONGRESS CATALOGING IN
PUBLICATION DATA

Sadler, Catherine.   Two Chinese families.

   SUMMARY: Depicts life in modern China by
focusing on the daily activities of two children
from different families.
   1. Family—China—Juvenile literature.
2. China—Social life and customs—Juvenile
literature. 3. China—Social conditions—1976
—Juvenile literature. [1. China—Social life
and customs. 2. China—Social conditions—
1976. 3. Family life—China]
I. Sadler, Alan, illus. II. Title.
HQ640.S23   951.05   81-2172
ISBN 0-689-30865-5   AACR2

Text copyright © 1981 by Catherine Sadler
Illustrations copyright © 1981 by Alan Sadler
All rights reserved
Published simultaneously in Canada by
McClelland & Stewart, Ltd.
Composition by The American Book/
Stratford Graphics, Brattleboro, Vermont
Manufactured by
American Book/Stratford Press
Saddle Brook, New Jersey
First Edition

To Max

ACKNOWLEDGMENTS

We would like to thank Mr. Malcolm Elliott for his invaluable assistance.

We are also grateful to the U.S.—China People's Friendship Association and Luxingshe (China International Travel Service) for their cooperation and aid.

Our appreciation to Mr. Chang Sung Chi of the Permanent Mission of the People's Republic of China to the United Nations, to Mr. Hsieh Ding Hui of Luxingshe, Peking, and to Ms. Huang Hsiu Chung of Luxingshe, Guilin. Professor Bernard Solomon of the Department of Classical and Oriental Languages at Queens College, New York, was of great assistance and we would like to thank him.

To the two families of this book, the Chengs and the Heus, our deepest gratitude and lifelong friendship.

Contents

Introduction

The people of China have traditionally called their land "the middle kingdom." This was because of their ancient belief that China was situated at the center of the universe. For hundreds of generations "the middle kingdom" was controlled by the upper classes who dominated and exploited the common people. At their head was the Peacock throne, as the royal house of China was known.

The emperors of the Peacock throne considered themselves divine and their nation superior to all others. But in the nineteenth century the Western powers laid claim to a number of Chinese ports. For the first time China had to face the harsh reality that it was no match for the modern armies of the west. The power of the royal house began to weaken. In 1914 Dr. Sun Yat Sen was able to lead an uprising which toppled the ancient Peacock throne.

For the next thirty years China underwent great internal strife. Different political groups struggled for power. Finally in 1949, the Communist Party, under the leadership of Mao Zedong, took over and proclaimed the People's Republic of China. This act is commonly referred to as "Liberation." The task ahead of Mao was great—to transform a backward, feudal nation into a modern, socialist one by the end of the century. By socialist he meant a classless society in which all are equal and none are exploited. The Chinese Revolution is the continual striving by the people to achieve this goal. Mao began a series of policies to change all aspects of Chinese life, from education and family roles to agricultural and industrial techniques. In 1976

Mao Ze Dong died and the leadership of the People's Republic of China was taken over by Hua Guo Feng, and more recently by Hu Yao Bang and Deng Xiao Ping.

The Cheng and Heu families of this book live in Guilin, a city of 200,000 people. It is located in the Guangxi Zuang Autonomous Region of southern China. These two families' lives reflect those of families throughout China. Like all families in China today they are personally involved in what they call "the Chinese Revolution."

1
The Cheng Family

Off one of the narrow sidestreets of Guilin lives the Cheng family. Their house was built by Mr. Cheng when his eight-year-old son, Cheng Kai Tiao, was born. Mr. Cheng built the house with his own hands—in the tradition of his father and his father's father before him. It is made of plaster and wood and shaped like a giant horseshoe, around a central courtyard. The two bedrooms, the family/dining room, the galley kitchen and the lavatory all open off this court. Other houses on the street have either more or fewer rooms, some are shared with a second family, but most look just like the Chengs'.

Mrs. Cheng, Kai Cheu,
Kai Weng, Mr. Cheng,
Kai Tiao and Kai Chi

3

As in times past, the courtyard is the center of family activity. Every morning the Cheng family can be found there. Mrs. Cheng and the two older girls, Cheng Kai Chi and Cheng Kai Weng, are usually busy at the corner water faucet with the family wash. Kai Tiao feeds the chickens and duck in the coop while his father sweeps the yard and helps hang up the wash. Only little Kai Cheu doesn't have a task. But when she is a bit older, she will be expected to pitch in.

When morning chores are done, the family goes for a mile run. All Chinese families are encouraged to exercise together. Some practise shadow boxing, an ancient form of exercise and concentration. But the Chengs all like to run, even on the briskest of mornings. They run slowly so that little Kai Cheu can keep pace with them. They always take the same route—down the alleyway, past the eight other houses so like their own, then right—out onto the broader street where bicyclists and pedestrians are hurrying to work.

the courtyard chicken
coop

There are never many cars about. Few people could afford to buy them, even if they were available. But there are plenty of bicycles. At any hour the streets are thick with them. The Chengs run on—past the herb shop where remedies can be found for everything from measles to a cold, past the fresh fruit store where they often buy their produce. Sometimes they pass their neighbors making early-morning purchases before work. They often wave or nod their heads in greeting, but they rarely stop. There just isn't enough time to chat. Everyone has to be at work or school by 7:40 A.M. and they must still wash up and eat breakfast.

Once back at home, the children and their parents take turns washing at the courtyard washstand. There is no hot running water and so they must heat the water on the kitchen stove before filling the washstand basin. Afterwards, the girls help braid each other's long hair. Cheng Kai Tiao fetches the eggs from the coop while his father heats the wok in their galley kitchen.

early morning
shoppers in Guilin

The kitchen is long and narrow and consists of a stone slab with a cold water faucet, a coal stove, and a shelf that holds their pots and pans and dried goods. The family eats together in the next room which they call the family/dining room. They eat at their one large table. Their six chairs are of different sizes and styles. The room has concrete floors and its walls are covered with paintings Kai Tiao has painted in his free time.

Although Mr. Cheng likes to cook, he does not always prepare the meals. At lunchtime, whoever reaches home first starts the rice. At dinnertime, it is the same way. Even Kai Tiao knows how to cook, although it is generally agreed his painting far outshines his cooking. Before Liberation in 1949, the women of the house prepared the meals and did the housework. Men worked, when there was work, while the women stayed home. Children rarely went to school, unless they were the sons and daughters of the very rich. In fact, few people in China could read or write before the Revolution. Since then, the

Kai Chi and
Kai Weng

people have worked together to change the past. With a population increasing by 15 million each year, they quickly realized that both men and women would have to work if they were ever to feed and educate the people, let alone improve the quality of life. But if women were to work outside the home, it was obvious they would have to be helped with child-raising and household chores. And so nurseries and kindergartens were set up to care for preschool children, and family members—be they eight or eighty, male or female—were encouraged to share household tasks. Today it is unusual to find a house in China where all its members do not help with the daily chores.

After breakfast, the Cheng children gather up their school books and place them in the satchels they carry across their backs as they walk to school. Both their parents own bicycles, but they prefer to walk with their children. Until this year, Little Kai Cheu's grandmother took care of her during the day, but now she goes to kindergarten.

*leaving for school
and work*

At 11:30 the family reunites at home. They eat their lunch and talk about their days. Sometimes, when there is enough time, they play a few games of Chinese checkers. But their lunch break usually passes too quickly and no sooner have they taken out the paper board than it is time to leave home once again.

Both school and work end at 5 P.M., but Mr. and Mrs. Cheng often stay late at work to participate in work-study session. Usually the children reach home first. After starting the rice, they play together in the courtyard. They have few toys or games, but a washboard, a stool, a length of rope make for endless fun. On coming home most nights their parents are greeted by the sound of their children's laughter.

Dinner is a simple affair at the Cheng house. Generally the meal consists of soup, steamed or fried vegetables, and rice. Meat is both scarce and expensive and so not a daily part of their menu. But there is plenty of food on the table and frequently they invite a neighbor to join in.

Once in a while the family goes to a film or the People's Park to hear an evening concert. It is more common to find the Cheng children in the family/dining room—a single lightbulb lighting the table at which they are all busy with that day's homework. Since bedtime is at nine P.M. there is rarely time left for an evening's outing, but they all love listening to stories. There are many nights when Kai Tiao and his sisters fall asleep while listening to a visiting neighbor tell of places he has been or the way things used to be long before any of them were born. On nights like these Mr. and Mrs. Cheng have to nudge the children awake and urge them to go to bed. But little Kai Cheu and not-so-little Kai Tiao sometimes refuse to budge and have to be carried into the bedroom that all four children share.

*the family/dining
room*

何家

2
The Heu Family

Not far from the Cheng house is the Guilin Medical College compound. It consists of a medical college, a nurse's training station, a hospital, a nursery, three schools, various stores, and a series of apartment buildings that house the compound's workers. In one of these buildings live the Chengs' friends, the Heus.

The Heu apartment is on the second floor—up a dimly lit staircase. Baskets and boxes line its sides. At the top is a landing filled with objects, everything from brooms and kitchen utensils to small chicken coops. To the

Mr. Heu, Heu Feng
and Mrs. Heu

left is a dark, wide hallway off of which are the apartments. On either side of the hallway are small kitchens, each with a faucet, a stove and a stone shelf. There are four such hallway kitchens before one reaches the Heus' door.

Beyond the door is their apartment. It is very different from the "luxurious" home of the Chengs. The room is large, perhaps twenty feet by twenty feet, and very neat. A large bed and dresser, a table with four chairs and two stools, and a cupboard filled with books crowd the room. A window and open screen door let light drift in from a narrow balcony beyond. Close by, a large painting both decorates a wall and hides the entrance to eleven-year-old Heu Feng's tiny room. It is no bigger than a closet and her twin bed and small desk completely fill it. But the Heus consider themselves very fortunate indeed. None of the other apartments on the second floor boast such a room.

Heu Feng's room

Everyday life in a small apartment differs in some ways from life in a classic Chinese house. There is no central courtyard for Heu Feng to play in. To cook and wash the family must go out into the dark hallway. The lavatory is shared by the second floor tenants and is all the way at the end of the hall. But in many ways the Heu's daily routine is similar to that of their friends. Like the Chengs, they rise at six o'clock each morning. They dress, make their beds and tidy their home. Then they go for a run around the compound. Often their next-door neighbors, the Fus, join them. Heu Feng and the Fus' two children have grown up together. The two families often share activities. They are like members of the family and Heu Feng thinks of them as such.

After their run, Heu Feng and her father gather eggs from their landing coop and start breakfast. Meanwhile, Mrs. Heu goes over to the compound store to buy groceries and household items. She is a staff nurse at the

MIANBAO   GAODIANBINGGAN

hospital and often doesn't have time to make such purchases during the day or after work.

After breakfast Mr. Heu clears up while Heu Feng and her mother do the wash. They hang it to dry on their balcony. Often someone calls to them from another balcony. Sometimes it's to see how things are going, but more frequently it's to gossip. News travels fast from one balcony to another. It is extremely hard to keep secrets in such an apartment building. But the Heus don't mind. The Chinese traditionally lived with their large families. Often three generations—including grandparents, great-aunts and uncles, cousins—all lived under one roof. Even today it is common for grandparents to live with their children and grandchildren. Such an arrangement is favored by the government. Families with grandparents are allotted larger apartments and the old are encouraged to teach the young about the "bitter past." In such homes the children rarely go to nursery school. Instead, their grand-

parents act as guardians and teachers while the parents are at work. The parents are free to concern themselves with work while the aged have an important and useful role in society. Heu Feng's grandmother lives with Mrs. Heu's older sister in a nearby town. Heu Feng would like her grandmother to live with them, but she knows she is of greater use at her aunt's where there are younger children. Anyway, there are many elderly people in the building —all of whom like to care for children and tell them stories of pre-Liberation days. In fact, with everyone in the apartment building so involved with everyone else, it is very much like the extended family of the past!

In the mornings, Heu Feng and her parents leave the apartment together. They don't have very far to walk since Heu Feng's school and both Mr. and Mrs. Heu's workplaces are located within the compound. Like the Chengs, they stop for lunch at 11:30, but sometimes Mrs. Heu is late. There are often last-minute emergencies at the hospital to attend to. So Heu Feng

and her father prepare lunch and amuse themselves by reading or painting while they wait for her. Mr. Heu is a professional painter for the college and teaches his daughter whenever there is time. Like Kai Tiao, she dreams of being a successful painter when she grows up.

In the evening, it is Mrs. Heu who prepares the meal. Being from Canton—a region famous for its cooking—Mrs. Heu prides herself on her cooking skill. She likes to prepare special regional dishes for her family and friends. She and Mrs. Fu often work side-by-side in their kitchens, concocting dishes that fill the hallway with the wonderful smells of fragrant spices. Then both families cluster around the dining table and eat heartily. After all home-work is done, they either play Chinese checkers or go out. The Heus try to see each new film or performance that comes to Guilin. Sometimes they even go back and see a favorite show twice.

By the time they get back from their entertainment it is usually past nine. After their long and eventful day they are weary and eager for bed. But tired as she may be, Heu Feng usually lies in bed, fighting back sleep. She tries to remember every detail of the performance she has just seen so that she can recreate it in her next painting. Usually she finds herself dreaming of Sundays when she and Kai Tiao often get together to paint. He prefers painting landscapes to people and scenes, but he always likes listening to Heu Feng's stories of the plays and films she has seen during the week.

學校

3
School

The Banyan Tree School, which Cheng Kai Tiao attends, was one of the first schools in Guilin Township. Long before Liberation in 1949 it was a British missionary school. An ancient Chinese banyan tree grows nearby. It is said to be over two thousand years old. The missionaries named their school after it and hoped their students would grow as erect and strong as the banyan tree.

Every morning the school's 1,100 students walk past it and into the central yard. Most wear multi-colored blouses with red scarves tied about their necks. Their books are carried in cloth satchels across their backs. Like

the Banyan Tree
students

Kai Tiao's house, the school is built around a court. The structure is made of brick and is two stories high.

The Banyan Tree School is a primary school with five grades. Students range in age from seven to eleven years old. The school is overcrowded, as are most schools in China. There are sometimes as many as five classes for each grade. Each class remains in its homeroom for most of its classroom work, while the teachers move from classroom to classroom teaching their particular subjects.

Kai Tiao's second year class is located on the first floor, directly off of the courtyard. The classroom is filled with old-fashioned wooden double desks. A large table at the front of the room serves as the teacher's desk. Behind it is a huge blackboard, above which are two photographs. One is of Mao Ze Dong, the late founder and Chairman of the People's Republic of China. The other is of Hua Feng, his successor.

The forty-six students in Kai Tiao's class sit erectly on their wooden benches. Each morning a monitor walks along the aisles to see that everyone is clean and well-groomed. When inspection is finished the students read aloud for twenty minutes. The practice of reading aloud is carried on throughout the school. On clear days, when the windows and doors are open, one can hear the voices of all 1,100 students raised in reading.

Kai Tiao's studies include Chinese language, arithmetic, common knowledge (history and geography), art, physical training and "political study." In political study students are taught about the communist system of government in which they live. It tries to instill in them the importance of serving the people in order to make a better life for all and stresses that it is better to help one another than to compete for honors.

Kai Tiao's first forty-five minute class is followed by a ten-minute exercise break. Rain or shine everyone piles out of their classrooms and into

the courtyard. Some students like to throw balls into the basketball hoops. But Kai Tiao and his three buddies, Hung Liang, Wang Lou, and Mao Pe Jin, prefer to play a local game in which one kicks a small puck into the air with one's feet. They rarely play with the girls.

After recess the students practise their eye exercises for five minutes. In every school in China children perform daily eye exercises, usually for five minutes in the morning and ten in the afternoon. It is generally believed that through a daily routine of massage and exercise the eyes can be strengthened and eye problems reduced. Few children in China wear glasses. Eye exercises are followed by two more classes, after which everyone goes home for lunch.

At 2:30 school resumes. Afternoon classes follow the same pattern as morning ones: a class, recess, eye exercises, and two more classes. Once a week Kai Tiao and his classmates spend their third afternoon period on a plot eye exercises in the afternoon. Her courses differ slightly. She studies Chinese language, political study, common knowledge, mathematics, physical training (which includes gymnastics and volleyball), music and painting. Unlike Kai Tiao, Heu Feng does not study each subject every day. For example, she studies Chinese language every morning but she has only two music classes a week. And so each day is a little different.

Heu Feng's school does not have a plot of land for students to work, but there is a workshop, run by the local factory. In it, students make paper and cardboard boxes. Production figures are kept on a blackboard at the front of the workshop. Each day's total number of boxes produced is recorded there. The workshop is paid by the factory for the boxes it produces satisfactorily. The money is then used to buy films, sports equipment and song-and-dance costumes for the school.

Chinese jump rope

eye exercises

of land behind the school. Here they study agriculture. They learn ab[out] such things as plant growth and the rotation of crops. Later, when Kai T[iao] finishes primary school and is in middle school, he and his fellow students [will] be expected to work on a commune, or people's farm, for at least two we[eks] each year. Many students spend years on communes after they finish mid[dle] school. Others go to the country during the harvest season to help with [the] crops. With a population of 900 million to feed, everyone in the Peop[le's] Republic of China, from the student to the doctor, must be concerned w[ith] food production.

Heu Feng's school in the Medical Compound is newer than [Kai] Tiao's. It does not have an unusual name or an interesting history. But [in] other ways it is very much the same. It, too, is two stories high and conta[ins] a central courtyard. It, too, is overcrowded. Heu Feng's schedule is just l[ike] Kai Tiao's—three classes and eye exercises in the morning, three classes a[nd]

Once in a while Heu Feng and her fellow classmates are taken on outings to nearby factories and communes. Everyone is expected to participate in odd jobs suitable to their age and experience. In this way they gain a first-hand experience of work. Such outings are usually organized by a group called "The Little Red Soldiers." This group is dedicated to the three goods —good health, good study and good productive work. All members wear its distinctive red scarf.

Each year older members of the group visit the lower grades to explain the purposes of the organization and to ask pupils to apply. The application must include self-criticism and comments from one's fellow classmates. To be accepted one must be clean, honest, a good student, and dedicated to helping those who are in need. Little Red Soldiers act as morning monitors, help solve problems and conflicts in the class, take schoolwork to sick class-

of land behind the school. Here they study agriculture. They learn about such things as plant growth and the rotation of crops. Later, when Kai Tiao finishes primary school and is in middle school, he and his fellow students will be expected to work on a commune, or people's farm, for at least two weeks each year. Many students spend years on communes after they finish middle school. Others go to the country during the harvest season to help with the crops. With a population of 900 million to feed, everyone in the People's Republic of China, from the student to the doctor, must be concerned with food production.

Heu Feng's school in the Medical Compound is newer than Kai Tiao's. It does not have an unusual name or an interesting history. But in other ways it is very much the same. It, too, is two stories high and contains a central courtyard. It, too, is overcrowded. Heu Feng's schedule is just like Kai Tiao's—three classes and eye exercises in the morning, three classes and eye exercises in the afternoon. Her courses differ slightly. She studies Chinese language, political study, common knowledge, mathematics, physical training (which includes gymnastics and volleyball), music and painting. Unlike Kai Tiao, Heu Feng does not study each subject every day. For example, she studies Chinese language every morning but she has only two music classes a week. And so each day is a little different.

Heu Feng's school does not have a plot of land for students to work, but there is a workshop, run by the local factory. In it, students make paper and cardboard boxes. Production figures are kept on a blackboard at the front of the workshop. Each day's total number of boxes produced is recorded there. The workshop is paid by the factory for the boxes it produces satisfactorily. The money is then used to buy films, sports equipment and song-and-dance costumes for the school.

Once in a while Heu Feng and her fellow classmates are taken on outings to nearby factories and communes. Everyone is expected to participate in odd jobs suitable to their age and experience. In this way they gain a first-hand experience of work. Such outings are usually organized by a group called "The Little Red Soldiers." This group is dedicated to the three goods —good health, good study and good productive work. All members wear its distinctive red scarf.

Each year older members of the group visit the lower grades to explain the purposes of the organization and to ask pupils to apply. The application must include self-criticism and comments from one's fellow classmates. To be accepted one must be clean, honest, a good student, and dedicated to helping those who are in need. Little Red Soldiers act as morning monitors, help solve problems and conflicts in the class, take schoolwork to sick class-

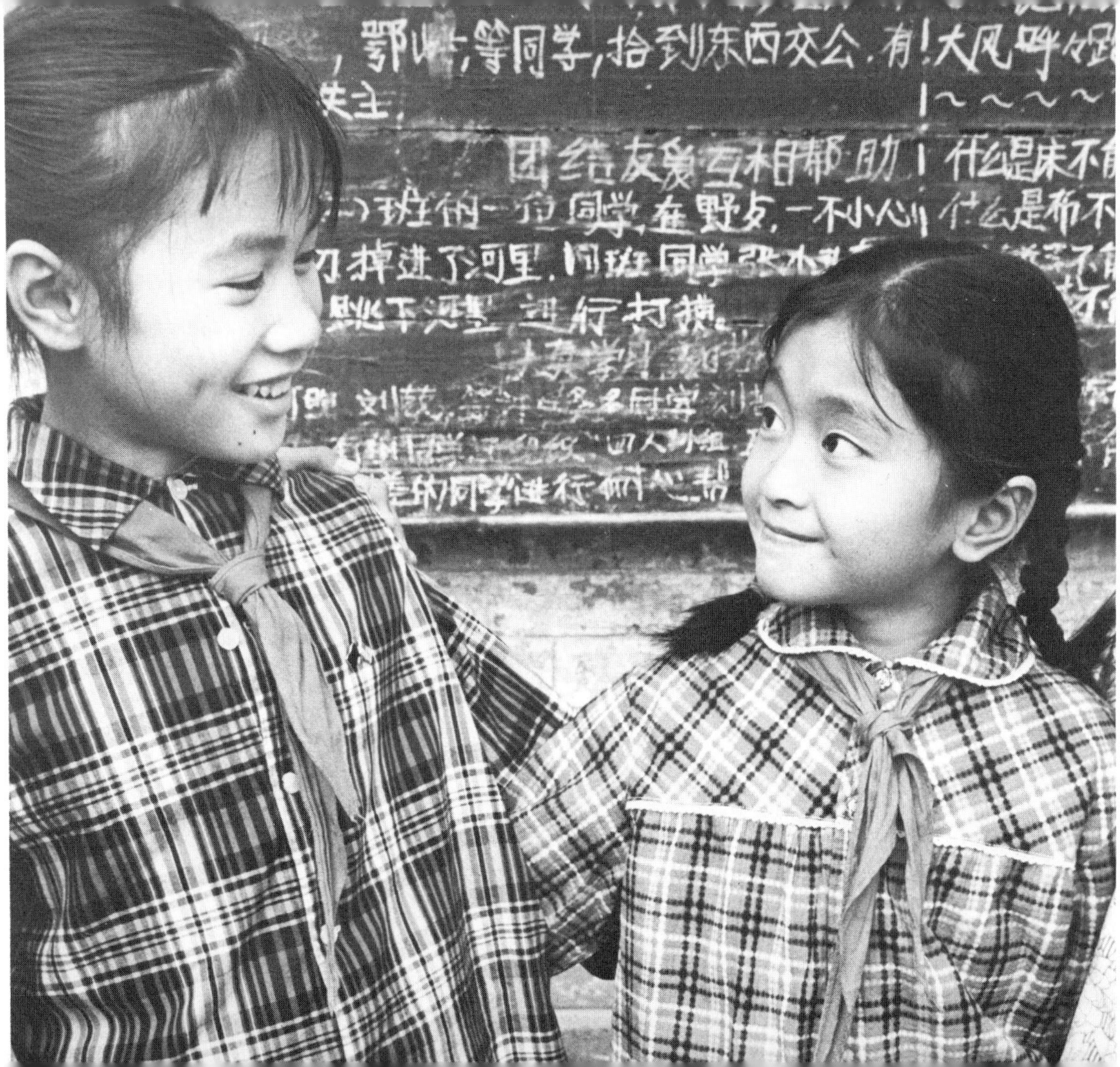
等同学，拾到东西交公．
团结友爱互相帮助
掉进了河里．同班同学
跳下河里，进行打捞。
同学进行耐心帮

mates, help students who are having difficulty in particular subjects and volunteer their services wherever needed. Everyone considers membership a great honor and all strive to belong. Even on Sundays and holidays, when their schools are closed, both Kai Tiao and Heu Feng proudly wear their brightly colored scarves to show that they are members of this student group.

工作

4
Work

Cheng Kai Tiao's and Heu Feng's parents go to work six days a week. Like everyone in China, they dress in pants, shirt and jacket. Although their jobs are different, their salaries are similar and each has the same work benefits— free dental and health care, after-work educational classes, free nursery care for their children and the option to retire at fifty-five years of age at two-thirds pay. Not everyone chooses to retire, but those who do usually turn their energies to volunteer work in the community or help in the home. But Heu Feng's and Kai Tiao's parents are young and retirement is still a long way off.

In the old society it is unlikely that either set of parents would have had an education or opportunities for interesting careers. Mrs. Cheng and Mrs. Heu would have been married off young—probably not to husbands of their choice. They would have had to live with the husband's family where they would have been treated like servants. Mr. Cheng and Mr. Heu probably would have worked the land for a rich landlord who took the best grain for himself. During drought and famine they would have been reduced to eating such things as roots and the bark of trees . . . as their parents and grandparents did so many times. But all four were born in the 1940s—a time of great upheaval in China. Old ways were being overturned. Drastic changes were being made at every level of society. No longer were landlords to dominate peasants, no longer did women have to marry against their wills and forsake their own families. Ways were developed to safeguard against famine

and drought. Schools, factories and communes were opened throughout the nation to educate and employ the people. Mr. and Mrs. Cheng and Mr. and Mrs. Heu were the first generation to truly reap the rewards of China's transformation from a feudal state into a modern, united, socialist nation.

As a child, Mr. Cheng was able to attend primary and middle schools in Guilin where he lived. After graduation he joined a construction crew and worked as a laborer, carrying bricks, laying mortar and operating cranes. Due to his ability to take charge and solve problems, he was eventually made a construction foreman. Today he oversees the construction of new apartment buildings in Guilin. During his work-study sessions he and his fellow workers discuss their weekly output and ways in which they can improve it. Over the years they have devised many plans for cutting down on waste materials and have improved machinery to increase productivity.

Mr. Cheng at a
construction site

Like her husband, Mrs. Cheng was born in Guilin. In school she excelled in mathematics. When she graduated she was chosen to teach geometry at a local primary school. She learned teaching skills on the job and was helped by the more experienced teachers during work-study sessions. After eighteen years she is still looking for ways in which to improve her teaching. She shares the hope of so many teachers in China that through their work more and more students will go into the field. Teachers are desperately needed to remedy the overcrowding that now exists in China's classrooms.

Mr. Heu was born in Vietnam, but his family moved back to China when he was small. He always loved to paint and studied art at middle school. After graduation he was assigned to Guilin's Medical College as resident artist. He could not have been happier. Guilin is famous for its beautiful landscape—painters from all over China come to paint Guilin's mountains and

Mrs. Cheng teaches
her third year class

rivers. Mr. Heu was able to live and paint in one of China's beauty spots while being of service to his country. As resident artist at the Medical College he paints diagrams and charts for the doctors' and nurses' classes. But his talents for painting scenes and landscapes are not wasted. He often paints posters and paintings to entertain and inspire the entire compound.

Mrs. Heu was born in the southeastern city of Canton, but her family moved to Guilin when she was a young girl. In Guilin she attended a special nurse's training middle school. When it was turned into a hospital and college, she remained on to work as a staff nurse. Because of the nature of her work, she is always on call. Sometimes she must give up her one free day, other times she is late for lunch or dinner, or misses them entirely. But this is typical of medical workers throughout the world and Mrs. Heu and her family adjusted to her schedule long ago.

Mr. Heu at the Guilin
Medical College

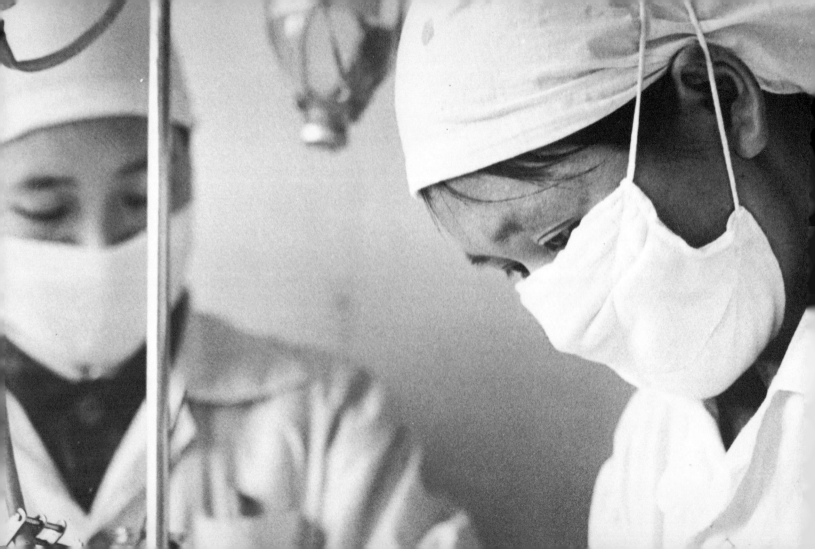

Neither Kai Tiao's nor Heu Feng's grandparents could read or write until they were adults. As peasants, the possibility of their children and their children's children being educated and having careers was an impossible dream. But in two generations that dream has been achieved.

Mrs. Heu assists an
operation

暇
日

5
Free Day

There is an ancient Chinese saying that "one can search many lifetimes to find a place more beautiful than Guilin." For centuries Chinese have traveled to Guilin to see for themselves the area's unusually shaped hills and caves. The curious shapes of the hills have always caught the Chinese imagination and there exist countless stories about their origins. Both Kai Tiao and Heu Feng—like all the children of Guilin—love the hills' and caves' intriguing names: Elephant Trunk Hill, Folded Brocade Hill, Seven Star Cave. They have all explored the caves where rock formations resemble exotic creatures

early morning in
Guilin

and glimmering lights create a magical atmosphere. But attractive as the folk tales and legends are, they know the answer to the question of the hills' origins is based firmly in science.

Millions of years ago Guilin was a sea bed, covered in limestone. Through the movement of the earth's crust the sea bed was thrust up and layers of limestone then formed hills. Wind and water chipped away at them to create the fantastic shapes that inspire their names.

For everyone who lives in Guilin, Sundays and holidays are a time to enjoy the natural beauty that surrounds them. The people's parks are always crowded with young and old . . . some strolling, some courting, some painting, some picnicking. There are often Sunday entertainments in the parks such as song and dance recitals, puppet shows and local exhibitions. The city streets are also full of activity. Many sidewalks are lined with amusements,

Sunday cyclists

everything from acupuncture demonstrations to rifle ranges. The shops are always crowded with shoppers busily buying special items for the evening meal which they plan to share with family and friends. Bicyclists leisurely ride their vehicles down the broad streets while on the river, junks and pole boats, called sampans, ferry people to and fro.

One of Heu Feng and Kai Tiao's favorite Sunday outings is to visit the local zoo in Seven Star Park. It is not very large but it does have a panda and a very friendly camel. Kai Tiao always likes to find a long bamboo stalk or sturdy twig and play tug-of-war with the camel. Another time they might sketch China's second national bear, the lesser panda, which actually looks like the American raccoon. Whatever they do, they always end up taking out their portable easels and painting what they have seen. Often they talk to each other about the differences in their work and how each can improve.

Both are very serious about their painting. Each is known in the area as an aspiring young painter and has exhibited work. In China it is a great achievement to be an artist. Both the Heu and the Cheng families are proud of their children's talent and try to help them in their endeavors. Heu Feng is tutored by her father, while Kai Tiao is taught by a well known local artist.

On clear days Kai Tiao and Heu Feng often go down to the river. The Likiang flows along the base of the limestone hills. It winds its way through Guilin to Yangshuo, a town fifty miles south of Guilin. From there it joins the Pearl River. The lime of its waters makes the Likiang crystal clear, reflecting the odd-shaped crags that loom high above like a mirror at their base. Because the water is so clear, one can see fish swimming below. Early in the morning fishermen stand in their pole boats, spear or nets in hand, watching and waiting. When the water is shallow, Heu Feng and Kai Tiao wade across to the opposite shore.

Kai Tiao and his tutor

Both of them try to paint the same scene from different angles and at different times of day. They are intrigued by the difference light can make as to how an object appears. For example, in the morning Camel Hill always looks like a lazy old camel sitting squarely on its haunches. But somehow in the afternoon, when the light is brighter, he looks as if he is standing up to take a long drink from the Likiang.

For both children, one of their fondest memories is when their two families took a boat trip to Yangshuo. The rolling green hills were dotted with flowers of every description and clumps of bamboo, shaped like giant feather dusters, grew on the river's banks. They passed boats of every description—some were fishing boats where families lived year-round, others were passenger boats like their own taking visitors and residents from Guilin to Yangshuo, some carried pieces of machinery and others were loaded high

a pole boat on the
Likiang

with local produce. At each bend in the river a new spectacular view came into sight. Kai Tiao and Heu Feng painted to their hearts' content. The paintings from that memorable trip still hang on the walls at home.

Someday Heu Feng and Kai Tiao hope to travel across the People's Republic of China to paint other regions—perhaps even to travel to far-off countries they have read about in books. But they both know there is much work to be done in their homeland and they may be called upon to take up some other type of work. Neither is worried about this possibility. They will be glad to work in whatever ways their country sees fit . . . and what better place to remain than in their beautiful Guilin.